THE NATIONAL POETRY SERIES
1984

IN THE SOLAR WIND, by Wendy Battin
(Selected by William Matthews)

THE PERSISTENCE OF MEMORY, by Mary Fell
(Selected by Madeline DeFrees)

BLACK DOG, RED DOG, by Stephen Dobyns
(Selected by Robert Hass)

GOD'S MISTRESS, by James Galvin
(Selected by Marvin Bell)

ARK 50, by Ronald Johnson
(Selected by Charles Simic)

In the Solar Wind

WENDY BATTIN

DOUBLEDAY & COMPANY, INC.
Garden City, New York
1984

Designed by Judith Neuman

Library of Congress Cataloging in Publication Data

Battin, Wendy.
In the solar wind.

(The National poetry series)
I. Title.   II. Series.
PS3552.A8315I5   1984   811'.54
ISBN 0-385-19384-X
ISBN 0-385-19385-5 (pbk.)

Library of Congress Catalog Card Number 83-20811
Copyright © 1984 by Wendy Battin

Printed in the United States of America

First Edition

Stars like gold tufts.
———— ———— *golden bees.*
———— ———— *golden rowels.*
Sky peak'd with tiny flames.
Stars like tiny-spoked wheels of fire.

Gerard Manley Hopkins, Diaries

ACKNOWLEDGMENTS

The Akros Review, No. 6, Fall 1982: "Letter to an Actor"

Attaboy: "Contra Dance"

Chiaroscuro: "Coffee," "Keeping House," "The Seasons Have Unwound," and "Ceremony" (under the title "October") first appeared in *Chiaroscuro*

Cincinnati Poetry Review: "The Dogs"

Corona: "Cassandra," "The Leper," and "Invention of the Phoenix." Originally published in *Corona*, Vol. 4, 1984

Epoch: "Waking"

The Georgia Review: "Christine Falls on the Road to Paradise." Originally published in *The Georgia Review*, Spring 1983

The Iowa Review: "The Lives We Invite to Flower Among Us" and "Letters from Three Women." Copyright © 1981 by the University of Iowa, *The Iowa Review*, Vol. 12, Nos. 2/3

The Nation: "Billy Goat and the Tree of Life" and "This World Begins on a Wharf." *The Nation* Magazine, Nation Associates, Inc., 1982, 1983

Poetry Northwest: "Cape Cod" and "The Lighthouse Has No Keeper"

The Seattle Review: "Astral Projection." Originally published in *The Seattle Review*, Vol. 4, No. 2, Fall 1981

Shankpainter: "Ghazal"

Tendril: "In the Solar Wind" first appeared in *Tendril* Magazine, No. 19

Vegetable Box: "Walking the Borders" and "Lullaby." Originally published in *Vegetable Box*, Spring 1981

Willow Springs: "Persephone Returns to Hades," "Maya at Equinox," and "Maya in Winter"

"Letters from Three Women" and "The Lives We Invite to Flower Among Us" appeared in *Extended Outlooks: The Iowa Review Collection of Contemporary Women Writers* (New York: Macmillan, 1982)

Diaries, by Gerard Manley Hopkins. *A Hopkins Reader*, selected and introduced by John Pick. Copyright © 1953 by Oxford University Press, Inc., New York and London.

Thanks also to the Fine Arts Work Center in Provincetown and to the MacDowell Colony, where many of these poems were completed.

Contents

I

II

III

I

Christine Falls
on the Road to Paradise

Remember how sunlight drills
its own road through a cloud?
So that through the sky
there is a tunnel of sky.

Water falls from the sun-struck
edge of the glacier. It has no
bones, it has no intentions.
The sheer air cannot divert it.

The masses of granite and greenstone
cannot reach it. Only the simple
force on the supple
body of water moves it

down to the flower fields
of Paradise: farewell-to-
spring, larkspur, shooting
star, on the summer slopes,

stonecrop, higher and pale,
mountain misery, whose five
white petals splay in a wheel
like Da Vinci's man.

4

Is he rolling somewhere,
dizzy but perfected—
into the fireweed,
into the monkey-flowers?

Or to Christine, who died here
or was born,
or only remembered by someone
making a map.

She has left
her name to a pillar
of water, her monument
stubbornly forgetful.

Paradise Lodge, Mt. Rainier

Astral Projection

I.

Each night my body leaves me, walks
to the brink of a city she imagines is yours,
though I tell her it's my place to wander, hers
to sink like an anchor through sleep.
I find her counting the lights that swim
below her, in the valley,
where thousands flip switches,
stroke gray cats. I cannot call her back.
And when she returns in the morning, stretches
out of her wake, I sense again
she has not found you.
It is not the old law of exile—just
the city rebuilding its walls,
this time to exclude her.

II.

To overlook the city at night
is to look at the sky: at points of light:
to look with the same fear of falling.
And each constellation a theory: connect the dots.
Out of this problem a building arises,
its random lights floating in the harbor,
its tenants peering into the world

like the drowned at a porthole,
their long hair streaming.
In the city the sky
rolls in and out like a tide,
on some nights remembered as it drains
away, on others
brimming among the rooftops as if they were piers.

III.

Only then do we know we've forgotten—mistaken
the electric lights in the park, each
a sufficient moon in its firmament
of leaves.
The trees glow as only the sky
holding the moon once glowed,
their lives uncovered like the heads of mourners.
But that is how grief in the city burns,
in commons where fear of the woods
is gone, where only the people harbor
death in the cultured forest;
where we are the ocean, the ground,
the sky and all our weather:
why we gathered here, and why we stay.

Billy Goat and the Tree of Life
after a statue found at Ur

What the Chaldeans saw
that set their hammers
against the original

gold is behind us. A goat
we assume is a god, because he stands
on two legs, as we do,

towers like a tree
against a tree. His forked trunk
grows as we do, out of two roots.

But the tree rises as only itself
from the ground. And so we have
composition, the tripod

on which a lens can be mounted
to stabilize vision.
God the goat raises

his hooves in the branches. The tree
branches, branches as far as
the valence of metal allows.

They saw this perhaps
watching the goats
that went among them on

four legs, even in the city—
the city, their latest idea,
like an upstanding

goat, that stumbled
forward on language and
barter, always out of step.

The weight passed from my
hand to yours might have been
a word that you'd carry

the length of the clay-banked
channels we would call streets,
while the goats

wandered everywhere feeding
on everything,
asking what nothing was worth.

Cape Cod

On the dunes, on Truro's backside, the clouds
open and close like gauze curtains (the yellowed
drapes that follow a woman from room to room
and keep her last colors from fading) lighting
and shading improbable contours. The dunes
mutter with gravity, against gravity, tilting
up oddly like concave lenses,
and would be glazed into lenses in fact
if the heat were greater.
Plovers, rain-spotted birds, have congregated
in the hollow.
They are posing as rocks,
the remains of a meteor shower.

To the east the Atlantic speaks more clearly.
Scrub oak, and clumps of marram grass sharing
a single root, like a life-line, explain
whatever coherence makes land into landscape:
a bargain, constantly haggled, between
provisional hills and green bullheadedness.
But here, half a mile inland, the weeds
have not held on; the ocean's
voice is confused by the wind in the random
chambers the dunes leave.

10

A woman walking here draws a curtain of sand
behind her. The crests
of the hill-waves, so sharp when the sun
glanced off them,
are raining a fine rain of sand.
When the woman passes,
the birds disclose their wings.

They scatter, piping into the air
like tongues from the Tower
of Babel, out over the dunes.

The Lives We Invite to Flower Among Us
Flower Beyond Us

> For just as that wild animal, if it shall have
> escaped and thus recovered its natural liberty, is no
> longer the property of its captor, so also the sea may
> recover its possession of the shore.
>
> —Hugo Grotius

Just as that wild animal, the sea,
is never in our midst, is constantly
our border, so also
a leopard, even in a zoo,
escapes us. He prowls
all our city's avenues, pacing
cage corner to corner, even
when we are most vigilant.

Set him free on the beach.
A body in a halo of senses,
he moves on the sand like water. The highest
wave casts down the shore like a spotted cat.
Nothing, our oldest lesson save one,
nothing is harder than water. The cat
on flat beach, the cat with no tree,
no ledge, as if caged,
cannot contain himself.

So also the thought containing the cat,
set in motion in a woman's
mind, a word
in a halo of sense. She makes
the leopard dark avenues
into the city of men, and then
she makes the seventh wave,
ending in foam just short
of the body poured out on the sand.
But even when she is
most circumspect, her mind

cannot contain itself, as a vase
may hold a flower but may not hold
itself. She loses the word
that strokes her into sense, that moving
cage and comfort.
The cat escapes
into the oldest lesson: no thing
is more yielding than water.

The woman rests
her mind in her body
in a halo of sense,
as if she were the sea,
and continent.

Saints Hover in the Windows

They have been shattered
and stitched with metal.

Green branch, gray colonnade—
their landscape resolves,
as if the world's kaleidoscope
had finally come to rest.
How they, in the morning, take

the world and pass it in:
azure pools on the floor,
on the blond pews.
They are curious, spread
with their open palms
through the leaded glass.

How they give back to the city
at night, fly like kites
in their stone sky and fall
opaque while the faithful are sleeping.

Who can name them?
Their faces are windows.

Their lives burn away
as the light passes through them.

Letters from Three Women

We are moving from state to state,
as they say of excited electrons, or

of water when it freezes
and sublimes,

or of the mind as it enters a drug
like an airplane.

When the letters bloom out of their envelopes
I think it must be spring,
remembering winter and the mailbox empty.
The pages collect on my desk, interleaved
like hands in a public oath. What
are we swearing to?

One has married her solitude,
wants a divorce.

One imagines that she
has not been understood.

One imagines she has.

The snapshot taken
through a fingerprinted lens records
identity and place: the smudge

floats in the doorway, a halo
whose saint has walked out.
One morning I watched from that beach
while a house rounded Long Point into the harbor.
Pennants, strung from the cupola
down to the barge, snaked in the wind and shot
the gulls through with panic.
The windows and doors had been boarded shut,
as if the house would founder if it woke.

You know me. I thought,
This is history: a house drifting sullenly
over the ocean.
Just look at the baggage we carry.

It docked at Macara's wharf for months,
waiting for cranes from New Bedford to lift it
bodily, as we all wait

in our rented rooms, or when
there's money, in apartments.
Today I receive you all in my room,

which dangles over traffic. The last one
huddled on a different city's ground,
under the weight of those
families I heard in the night,
like Hansel in the oven, listening.

I hear, for example, that lessons learned
drunk are best remembered drunk,
that the mind
knows this on the ocean and something
else at the kitchen table over coffee;
and think
especially of the humpbacks, who pass
their songs from ocean to ocean in
intricate barter.
                        Some days
I read you between the mailbox and my door,
the way we've eaten whole meals cooking them.
Is the ocean just a mind with a tune
running through it? The sun here

travels into an ocean
so monstrous we call it
peaceful, adrift on the land.

Ghazal

The wall erased, its graffiti hang in the air:
We are open all night, like old men's windows.

The trees creak in the cold wind:
doors that rarely open, opening.

A man's borders include the axe he swings, the branch
it splits. The cold peal traveling elsewhere.

And who opens like a door cannot
say who might enter, or question

the gifts we make to morning, boosting
the last of our loves over the wall.

The Apple Is a Rose: October Fair

Apples litter the ground.
The world accumulates.

I am hungry, and in the tent
of apples there is no air to breathe
but the breath of apples. I have
no money among the baskets of Winesaps,
Delicious, Golden
Mongols and hybrid
experimental apples.

An ant might circumnavigate
an apple and find no food.

This hunger must not be confounded with
the fingers that trace the apple's skin
or with the delirium of scent.

The skin of an apple is a meal
made only of exclusions.
Lost in a cloud of apples, gathered
into the rose I invent

a mathematics for what I cannot
reach: picture
the lines of perspective,
receding like wires on which are strung
red beads.   Inside the rose,
this is the portrait of distance.

Picture the carnival tent,
that blowsy canvas rose that holds the scent
of bushels of every apple of our knowledge.
Picture the theoretical ant,
his incessant exploration.

There is no one to tell him to stop.
This is the time that hunger's clocks
keep in the heart of the rose, in hunger.

Cassandra

To speak at all I must pose
on the highest step, and squander
a week's ration of breath.

Bird squawk. Wind wash. You hear
what I say is abundantly
air, more rare

in space than the matter
with us, and the state.
The city rolls over the earth

like fog, without landing like fog
in beads on the grass first morning.
We tried mourning our own

passage into still life
because we had learned the word:
to mourn: the warm

pressing together of lips at its
beginning, and the tolling
of *our* in our throats on its way

to denial, *N.*
Who imagined the truth
was separate from its unfolding?

I've seen a ring around the moon,
as perfect as Euclid
and just that empty.

It held a huge dead world, cold light—
and the god who wanted my body
has taken my tongue.

The ring.
The moon nested there
threatens to hatch.

Lullaby

The woman in the next apartment trailed
home with a lover last night: soundtrack of keys

and voices in the hall, and through the wall
later the universal male moan, swinging

open the gate in the throat. What goes unheard
is seduction, and I thought of you

again, your body rangy among the voltmeters
and consoles. How accurate our backs are, turned,

triangulating the distance between those most
foreign objects, each other. This is a state

the priests called *immanence*, more blessèd
in the Godhead's privacy than here, in this

room of manifest tables. And this is in praise
of simple lust: the bodies pray themselves into

encompassing light. The brain thinks *not now,
not then,* but the bodies

think as computers think,
when the current runs through them.

Ceremony

Three stragglers, Canada
geese headed north interlace
their lines of flight as if
to braid their intentions
together. Three? Your leisure, mine,
and another. We talk over wine as
if we kept no secrets. The geese
locate their north, fly
out of their knot. The inlet
now reflects a world

quieter in its spectrum: oaks,
sky, the high cirrus washed
with a mute green:
as it should be, the water
that marries them visible.

Insomnia in Tucson

The moon glares down and the desert glowers back,
reflecting on its future. Foothills rise into
mountains, mountains rising toward the moon, worn
down with waiting. When I woke from my dream of water
this is what I saw: the green veil parting,
the fabric of coat and the fabric of flesh
torn, the body dressed for patience in its durable
bones. Even the light is weary, from the sun
to the moon, to the earth, now lifting
weakly from a white shoulder. Such a long sleep
to be broken before sunrise, no sound
but a remnant of waves, not here, not here, like all
that I've carried, carried too far.

Persephone Returns to Hades

This is no forced retirement; my job
carries me all summer to
the adits of abandoned mines.
You ask me how many ways there are
of slipping into the earth.
There's always a new route.

Like this: I wade
into the rain.
Like this: I take the subway.
I call it a career, as one careers
down a slope on skis.
      Forgive me.   These meetings
are awkward as courtship.

The truth: I've come
through my mirror,
as always.   I turned and saw
everything reversed, the leaves
on the brown tree growing
greener through the window.
I peered in and thought,
This is a room I remember being
a woman in.

This is the way I held my head.
And so I spend my winter
here, in your arms, watching
for skylights, chimneys,
the way out.

The Lighthouse Has No Keeper

I thought, tonight off Land's End nothing clicks.
The Bay is the same old kettle of fish,
geologically speaking.
A buoy rocks
under a cormorant, ringing
position.
                    The black
fish-eater hangs its ragged
wings to dry, *spread-eagle* though
an eagle's wings spread out like entire
kites, unlike the kites on broken
frames the voracious
ancient cormorant angles out.
The snake-necked black
bird in the dark appears
only one second out of every thirty,
when the lighthouse sweeps it.
Its shape
splays like the fossil half-bird,
Archaeopteryx pressed in rock,
a feathered lizard with a toothy grin.

The lighthouse has no keeper, has
a clock of gears the mechanic
visits monthly.   And

in fact the lighthouse clicks,
somewhere in its shell, behind
its diamond eye.

                        I am mistaken.
Somewhere in the Bay a dolphin
clicks.   Its word in the water
is 31 meters long, a long word
uttered quickly.
I think the lighthouse has no keeper. The keeper
ticks in its sleep and pulls

the light in a broad, sensible circle
all night long.
Thought, thought
is hard as a diamond
egg to hatch from.
                      The cormorant's
an old bird: pressed through rock it comes
out the other side,
goes fishing, hangs its wings to dry
in the lamplight.   Everything clicks.

Waking

A slow sine wave into day,
surfacing from the aquarium.

The path your eye
insists on,
vertical
to a hushed sweep,
gathering the room into
a known geometry.

II

The Seasons Have Unwound

and will not circle back again.
You pad like a cat through the changing
woods, trying to save what's left before winter
swallows the red leaf, the yellow, the last
finger of the creek that passed
through August. It's the question
you've answered and never answered:
What would you save from a burning house?
You clutched at *my daughter,*
and the key to the safety deposit,
where the will is. Or you guessed
an armload of books, your grandmother's
dulcimer. The first time the question
hypnotized you, suddenly wealthy.

Once I hoped I'd save only
myself, naked and untraceable.
I wanted to stand in the mob of the curious
gathered at the curb and watch
the uniforms of recognition kindle and smoke,

to be absolved of owning.
The present is burning.
I know myself only
by what I've discarded, a vagrant's
inventory of ashes.

The trail is wild with an old palette;
you kick away horse chestnuts,
little hibernacles. And at a rail fence labeled
Private Property, you stop, smoke,
ponder the bread you are going home
to bake, so happy to be turned back
that your muscles hum
with you through the dead woods.

Maya at Equinox

Delicate balances have their points of
oscillation composed of a steel knife edge
working on agate planes.
                    —*Orr's Circle of the Sciences*

If this were the old days she'd
be spinning wool: the last day of
summer, the first
of something she won't name
quite yet, though
the sumacs know, the chicory
poised in their final

reticence know, and name it to themselves
while the sunlight draws its blade
across them. Today the wool
wouldn't stick to her fingers, tacky
with sweat. Nothing new has sounded,

but something old is quiet, suddenly;
she opens her closet, full
of woolen coats from sheep
a hemisphere away.

*

The book she takes from the shelf reads hiber-
nation, Hibernian, *hiver*. The air
still Septemberish: whether
to carry a sweater plagues her for once
more than the planet, that spins
for once not cockeyed.

On the street she repeats the word
equinox.
Through the door of the word,
a hallway.
At the end of the hall, a blue stone.
She's on her way to meet
a man who isn't her lover: her husband.
She spins
a curtain of heavy wool.

*

A woman hangs a blue wool curtain
before a stone.
Nothing new has sounded,

but something old begins to speak,
talking her down the sidewalk as if
she might only fly by instruments
through the clear air. This is the day
the year rocks in its balance,
the equal night. She spins

as the planet spins her. The edge between day
and night, never so honed: split
by the blade she walks both roads, down
the street, down the hallway, toward winter.

Letter to an Actor

Dear D___,

You ask me, *what news?*
I can tell you my days are ground
so fine that they build up
like dunes, then shudder
gradually into the craters
under the wind.
And the light in this room
could be ocean light: blue,
its shadows accidental.
But this is a city
washing around me.
The punctual tides are buses
bawling through rain.
How can I read this summary
of roles you have taken and
tell you I
have none, not even myself?
A friend walks in with his
day's grief and first
I feel how soft his jacket
has become with such
long wearing. Only later,
how warm the body, old spendthrift,
throwing off heat.

Things that have been cut loose
collect in this quiet: the man
rapt on the sidewalk who tells me
the stars are regrouping, and
at a bus stop, the woman.
She has carried her story along
this route for years.
She has waited so long to
speak that the words
come out yellow and brittle,
in danger in the acid air.
She says that they're coming to take
her away, but she is not there. Henry,
Maria, the doctors are not doctors,
neither are the children
children.
                    She cannot guess
I do not know them,
her world is so naked
and the bus is so late.

I am not lonely. This could be
after all a morning you would recognize,
off-season, if you lie in bed
in a white room,
your last speech forgotten, the next
script shut on your dresser.

Keeping House

Domestic, as the young cat puzzles
out the windowpane: somehow the trees,
the diving birds, are cold and flat to touch.
The sill is a ledge in the cliff face
where the cat suns and grooms her
hunger, and murmurs at a bird,
as if she is so in love that her voice
grows small when she speaks of it.
Her body gathers like a thunderhead.
Her shadow travels over the glass
and again she remembers the riddle
and forgets. Behind her I'm keeping
house, with the same concentration:
sometimes I hold it, sometimes I let it
go, while the walls play their own
quantum odds, and keep out the cold.

Walking the Borders
for R.L.

THE FALLS

We are washed in sound,
hollow as flutes.

We are flying, our shadows are flying
to Tucson in an old man's camera,
even now; set
here at the falls' throat
to give scale to the natural
staircase. He will say,
Those shapes are two women, climbing.
He said,
Don't move. Don't turn around.

Late dawn: it comes
almost at noon in the land's deep pockets.
A shadow splits my face so cleanly
one eye is scalded,
the other dark. The water is a ribbon,
anchored below and above.
And the mist:

This is chop-vision,
dismembered light, rising from impact.
You stroke the veined rock
like a man's back.
We did not come to be photographed.

THE CLIFFS

I want to leave my shadow among these rocks,
like a statue,

as I have left you silent
by the streambed. By now she has entered the earth,
your mother, as she tried to before:
she jumped and found it
closed against her, but now
it is open.

And you have come into the earth, not to talk,
not to touch, not to answer
the letters or breathe in the flowers. I've come
not to think of you here. Hear:

I recite: *my shadow's
a hole in the light,*

*the disciple the sun skips over
in its laying on of hands.*
In the desert it would be priceless,
costing me everything.

In this canyon the shadows are stone.
Here: the mime gathers eggs
from a neighbor's coop. *For you,*
I grin. Hold them up to the sun
and they disappear.

PHLOGISTON

Of the campfire we think: oxygen
marries dry juniper, violently,
atom by atom. What is gained
by this bright union,
ash, smoke, our dinner of fried trout.
                    The alchemist
thought of fire: *something is lost*.
Phlogiston.   The igneous
humor, the wood's
escaping soul.

As the soul is lost, in a bad bargain.
As the soul is stolen, by a camera,
   by the naming of a private name.
As the soul is thrown from a high window.
It rises from impact.

You stir the fire.   We breathe
juniper smoke, oxygen,
adding the gases to our blood.

44

THE GALLERY

The moon is collapsing, phase
by phase. Its light
populates the cliffs
with statues, still
and gesturing.
Your face, my hands
are chalk, are plaster.

Your dream: you turned
the last of a thousand pages
of a book set down
in your own round hand, and read
there is nowhere left to wake to.

I claim that we haven't slept. I claim
that the statues in the cliffs collapse
with the light, phase by phase:
   in their decay they beckon, turn
   their sculpted backs,
   revolve.   We
haven't slept. We have
no need to wake.

Coffee

Over coffee I think of him.
He has overheard this rain, or he rains
himself out of sleep, not knowing
what wakes him. He sways
in the kitchen and blinks, one match
flaming past his fingers.
The water in its black kettle
a bird in its covered cage—
a blind where agitation can dissemble
calmly. And the earth-black powder
just ground. A cup of mud, he calls it.
He is careless with his naming
and does not know, even after
coffee, when he tells some truth
and when he lies.
Does he switch on the radio? Does he
turn off the news and listen
instead to the plumbing's
bad digestion? Today I am
not in that room, and cannot say.
Coffee, black coffee. How are my nerves?
The first cup is steady, the second
still as a pond in a cave.
The third begins to stir in my hand,
small mammal at the end of hibernation.
This is a morning like any other,
and here is a way of waking
forewarned into its bitter warmth.

Maya in Winter

1.

For magic, four tools: the wand, the sword,
the pentacle, the cup. She must learn
their elements one by one,
be the patient woman who
turns to earth, the screaming woman
who drowns in air.
And in fire—in fire—
she starts off with water, thinking
how gently the riddles will ride
in solution.

2.

His camera, her beach. After the flashbulb
the eye remembers: a blue ring blind
at the center. Or is it the sun at noon,
low on the water this far north
in winter? She imagines for
once she's been caught with her eyes
open, but what did she see?
Everything that floats:
scallop boats, gulls
folded on the water
or unfolding; their cries
delay in the air, the ear, after
the birds wheel on.

She tries to hold her eyes to the white
line where the sky and the harbor
meet, where the blind circle settles.
She turns her head and it disappears;
it is the sun.

3.

As if her days were program music,
as if her instrument could be
tuned by the large hands that float
over her in sleep, lighting
like water, she watches, erases,
raises her cup. She could open
this film to the light, and the darkness
it remembers as form
and the passage of her body
would dissolve, so, into what she sees
here: the flat sheen of water,
light watered and thin.
She might begin again, as this bay
in December, unwitnessed.
Everything that floats
is an apparition. She sees
much, holds nothing, and soon
the fleet will sail through her, trading
in fire, in earth, in air.

Contra Dance

1.

I have worded my days like a careful
resignation, and you are accepting,
accepting. Your face
is clear as good whiskey, telling me
lies; what I hear
spins my nerves to a web
of sleep, where we lie
almost gracefully.

2.

Tonight we are rich.   Our steps
nailed the city streets together, corner
by corner. We can consult this map
forever, snaked between cars and starred
with restaurants.   We had

more pockets than hands,
and chose them well for every pose
and swagger, like dinner
forks at a formal table.   We had
more words than tongues,
and sent them off humming
the right tunes.   We lie

3.

almost gracefully   the theater lobby
the sheathed women   the linear men
like a contra dance   like pinwheels   only
children dodging among us like sheepdogs.

And if at home I bristled like an electric cat?
And if the twice-worn necklace snapped
and if your face
flew past mine in the mirror like
a foreign flag?   We have
        our cash in the bank, and in our cheeks
our careful, diplomatic tongues.

50

It Snows Out of a Clear Sky
for C.E.C.

Like the chemist's beaker of tricks,
the air: there is nothing there,
and then the spontaneous white
generation of winter in Tucson.
It fills the dry arroyos, caps
the hydra cactus, gathers
in blades on the alien
palms of this desert.
What is the *it* that snows,
hiding in the wings of language?
The snow that can be named
is not the snow
touching the saguaro lightly along
its spines,
jamming the eight-track brains
of the highway tarantulas.
The woman from Los Angeles whispers,
so that's what it looks like,

as what she's learned to recognize
in books as death or the spiral
into silence falls
piecemeal before her.
It snows, as if someone had nudged it
and said,
Talk, or they will not listen.

Invention of the Phoenix

Now for once it is the real bird annulled in flames;
the one we have built goes on breeding.

The phoenix is false,
as a word or a friend
is false. Remember, we made it
from pieces of bird and the idea of fire,
from a bird and our confusion:
      that what is warm can burn.
      That there is an exchange
      in which this is the currency.

And our confusion about the bird
behind its wall of flight: that we
      are sundered by the third dimension;
      that we climb
      only the ladders we see; the bird
      climbs in transparency.

And with the fire: that it comes
      from the other side of the wall of matter.
      It appears to all the senses. We
      have asked it to live among us with
      the dog, the ox,
      and it has refused us.

It is only that we are confused.
We make firebirds, angels, and a bird
with a life span the length
of memory, which burns, and burns again.

The Leper

They gave me a bell
in place of a husband.
He tells me one word.
All morning while everyone
ambles the street
(they circle me
as if I were a fine lady
in a wide skirt)
he tells me, *sweet*.

My mother told me,
"Your skin is like milk.
You will marry."
She is gone. I have grown
so white I can answer
the moon. When we're alone
my bell whispers. When someone
comes near me, he shrieks.
Oh, he is jealous.

The Dogs

are pacing our yards
like sentries.   They yelp
clear across night to each
other, planning.
They shiver.   The virus
in each of their glinting minds
connects them.

The dogs
wheel through the park.
Already the lawn has grown a tongue
inside their rim of teeth.
It pleads in a green language: Close
your mouths while you chew!
Cover your bare
grins with your paws, be civil,
be mild, be mild.
The dogs hurl forward,
intent on their leader's
tail, invoking
the moon, their chalk Madonna.

They are calling down snow
in the desert, earthquakes,
raking up fields
of tempting bones.   The dogs
all dream like early Christians:
their teeth prepare
for the last day.
And what if I dream every night
that my flag is a tail, angry
and useful?
The dream connects.
The stiff hairs exclaim.

For Jean Valentine
MacDowell Colony 1983

Only strike the log
and the fire explodes in it:

beneath it the coals repeat
the catalog of forms the planet

sleeps through: red mesas,
black doorways into the glowing

city, bright masks rehearsing
the possible, the remembered:

this fire eating wood is the earth's
long dream of itself in a small brick

cave, in this cabin framed by January
birches: the living drink light

and the dead give it back
as flame; this book you've left here,

inscribed *with thanks
as always* for the world's

unaccountable shelter,
and your messengers

inside it,
calling the sleeper awake.

58

This World Begins on a Wharf

shy of midnight.
Under a moon that is almost
full. Yes, shy.
Its light skims a shiver
over the bay,
the light chill

of cold hands.
From here the world purls off
in all directions:
up, into stars,
Orion as always sharp
in the chaos of sparks;

forward, into the bay,
where the sound water beats
out of its body
rushes in, where a still
thick shadow is nothing,
or is the breakwater;

and down, the world stilted
on pilings, over
pale sand, now covered by
some afterthought of the bay,
now revealed,
a screen where the moon

throws timbers, doctored
blueprints, manic carpentry.
There are other bearings,
poor compass. Their names
dissolve into number, the numbers
divide like cells.

This world has just begun
and it fills them all:
breakers, dark storefronts,
panes of glass pooling
the light the length of a narrow
street, what the woman

on the wharf sees abruptly.
Her short hair caught
in a gray scarf,
her hands clumsy in gloves.
She sees so quickly, hears
so much with her skin, her blood,

that all this time her mind
is full of the last world,
the one she left when she stepped
absently up to the wharf
and found herself here.

III

In the Solar Wind

There is a sleep that tells every
dream as a nightmare: the figures rise up
in a locked room, and it is the world.
And there is a sleep of open windows,
where all dreams unwind
in golden light: clear tea
with the scent of almonds.
If there is something to look on
that does not waver
like mountains in the mirror of a still lake,
like the outline of trees in a light wind,
I have not seen it.
If there is waking.
Here in the thick
afternoon, I do not remember.

   *

Love, here is golden tea
in a glass cup. It is hot,
a flashing cylinder.
Hold the cup still and look in:
the future is there,
but not in a Rorschach of leaves.
Steam rises from the tea,
and what begins in this room
continues. To the molecules
every wall is a window.

*

The table he sets the cup on becomes
a story about a table:
It has four legs.
And another:
She rested her head on the table.
And another:
He sat at the table and wondered
if she would appear.

He remembers the table and sets down his cup.
  the liquid is sweet, and
  afterwards, almonds.
The story of the tea fills the air.
It is not finished,
not even in the next room.

  *

What does the table become for the child
crouching under the table?
A dungeon, a warren, the oak-grain
stormy an inch from the eye:
the privacy of narration, the
mechanics of hiding.

*

I am sleep, from which everything falls
as the dream rises up.

You cannot hold me,
not even in your strong arms.

I cannot hold you,
though the story might hold us.

One of us chooses to leave,
or what we are chooses:

we have chosen a world
that splinters and shifts,

from molecule to atom
to particle to quark.

Our substance sinks
into its fractured wealth

while we are left behind
in the poverty of our bodies.

*

He stares out the window
past the blue lake
into black woods
and does not see her coming.
There is the path she would take,
brown needles and earth
through the green grass.
He sips his tea and thinks of sleep,
and imagines her sleeping.

*

I could tell you my love is divisible
into need and desire.

That need reduces to past,
desire to present.

That the past is circumstantial,
the present a problem of engineering.

He sets down his cup and wanders
away from the window, into
the privacy of remembrance,
the mechanics of excuse: *when
I was a child*, he begins, and there,
where no one can find him,

the maps unfold in a small boy's hands:
the states, the pastel countries,
the earth—each sheet
drawn from a greater distance,
as if that were knowledge.
The last shows the planets
careening on the solar wind,
the sun's ionic breath.

     *

The province where this story unfolds
is a sheet of blue paper.
Brown lines indicate mountains.
The stars of the cities are black,
though they give off light.
In this country a law was uncovered:
we will never need more than four colors
to mark off our borders.
One of them is green.

     *

The pale blue is water,
a foreign country.
He knew he had no right to be
so happy, seeing her
floating in a clear sleep.
And so he stopped.
He did not see her coming
down the needle path.
He did not see her at all.

*

When the story has been well told
all tasks are simpler. We have built
so many empty houses; we have made
the roads that lead back to them broad.
When your hand moves to stroke my hair
what is the distance you travel?

*

I open the chest and find it empty.
I open the door and the light

is aimless in the room and settles nowhere.
I open the book and wait

for the story to begin.
It will take our present and make it pass.

*

She is sleeping, he thinks,
and then he can reach her: his fingerprints
on the air, on empty space.

She is sleeping, like dice in his hand:
twelve chances.

She is sleeping, like a cue ball:
a problem of vectors, complex but foreseen.